From the Series 'Martial Art of Business'

THE ULTIMATE GUIDE TO
Mastering your Business
& your Competitors

JAMES EDEN

Acknowledgements

Sun Tzu's Art of War is reputed to be the oldest military treatise in the world. The great work of Lionel Giles in his landmark translation from the Chinese in 1910 is acknowledged. This translation is freely available in the public domain in the USA.

The Martial Art of Sales © James Eden 2019

ISBN: 978-1-922264-59-6 (paperback)

Cataloguing-in-Publication information for this title is listed with the National Library of Australia.

Published in Australia by James Eden and InHouse Publishing.

www.inhousepublishing.com.au

Printed in Australia by InHouse Print & Design.

> *" All men can see these tactics whereby I conquer, but what none can see is the strategy out of which victory is evolved."*

Introduction

Ancient Chinese War Lord, Sun Tzu, is universally acknowledged as one of the greatest strategists of all time. Now, these ancient principles have been specifically translated and written for Sales Professionals wanting to win in the marketplace through superior execution.

Uniquely aligning an ancient wisdom to your business strategy, the Martial Art of Sales is a comprehensive marketing strategy workbook that delivers an arsenal of sales tools to outmanoeuvre the enemy in a competitive marketplace.

The Martial Art of Sales helps you gain a clear understanding of the marketplace competitive absolutes and how to train and position your sales team and their activities to maximize gain and minimize risks.

Apply the Martial Art of Sales business strategies to your on-line business and out-think competitors around the globe. Analyze your customer base and your competitors to target your markets with pinpoint accuracy.

The marketing strategies outlined in the Martial Art of Sales can be your lethal weapon when planning your next hard hitting campaign. You hold in your hands a comprehensive, readable and easy to use sales training workbook that will strategize you and your team to grow and prosper in the local and global marketplace.

Sun Tzu, the Martial Art of Sales is your best weapon in the battle for commercial and financial success.

You will learn to compete with strength and honour, to sidestep your enemies and to render them useless.

Are you ready to commence your training in the Martial Art of Sales?

Table of contents

Chapter One
Planning 1

Chapter Two
Marketplace Engagement 5

Chapter Three
Planning Campaigns...9

Chapter Four
Resource Formation 14

Chapter Five
Force 17

Chapter Six
Weakness & Strength 21

Chapter Seven
Competitive Activity 26

Chapter Eight
Ten Variables 31

Chapter Nine
Sales Team Maneuvers...34

Chapter Ten
Market Formation 37

Chapter Eleven
9 Market Engagement Risks 42

Chapter Twelve
Disruptive Attacks...48

Chapter Thirteen
Using Intelligence Providers 51

The original translation of Sun Tzu's Art of War 56

> **" "** *Unhappy is the fate of one who tries to win his battles and succeed in his attacks without cultivating the spirit of enterprise; for the result is waste of time and general stagnation.*
>
> *Hence the saying: The enlightened ruler lays his plans well ahead; the good general cultivates his resources."*

Chapter One
Planning

Battle in the marketplace is a great matter to a business. It is about survival and growth.

It's about pure Darwinism – survival of the fittest, elimination of those not so strong, and new growth based on new ecosystem or marketplace dynamics.

Sun Tzu said there are five factors to consider and make decisions about; Way, Heaven, Ground, General, Law

- The Way is about having the same approach to thinking as that of those who are superior to the ordinary person. The Way describes the people's loyalty to the cause with no fear of what lays ahead. The Way is about organizational alignment.
- Heaven describes the absolutes of competition – there is no in between; only black and white – slow market pace and fast market place and the changing ebbs and flows of markets.
- Ground is about competitive positioning in the arena of the market place and the operational risks associated with engagement.

- General describes the way in which the mind is applied; particularly wisdom, credibility, sincerity, courage and executional discipline.
- Law is simply the operational organization to efficiently and effectively execute in the marketplace.

In order to win in the marketplace, the leader must know how to master all five factors; including knowing the status of all five factors at all times.

The successful organization must;

- have alignment of purpose and objectives
- have a leader with ability
- a clear understanding of the competitive absolutes and how to position sales execution activities to maximise gain and minimise risks
- clarity in organizational execution
- a sales & marketing team that is strong and well trained
- and a clear reward system that has positive and negative consequences

With those six factors, you will clearly know what winning in the market place is, as you will clearly know what loosing in the market place is.

The leader who uses these principles to continuously evaluate market place activity will gain market share. The organization must do what is necessary to keep this leader.

The leader who chooses not use these principles and/or chooses not to continuously evaluate the market place will lose; and should be removed as soon as is possible.

Factor advantages from gathered market intelligence into current known market dynamics and with respect to competing forces for the allocation of resources; and then create focus into market place activities based on calculated advantages.

Competitive market place engagement is in the alignment of deceptive and advantageous thinking amongst all competitive personnel.

- Build and ensure your capability but show the opposition that you lack capability
- Ensure all competitive people and processes are active, but to the competition appear to be inactive, slow, unresponsive
- Make sure the market and customers know you are close to them but appear to distant in the eyes of your competitors
- If your competition has a competitive advantage, then cleverly arouse hope that they may succeed
- If the competition appears confused, act swiftly to capture their market share/customers
- Prepare for any activity from relatively larger competitors that may have an impact on your activities
- If your competitor is much stronger than you, then avoid them
- When your competitor is angry - interfere, interrupt, inconvenience and throw them into disorder
- If the competitor is humble (not arrogant or assertive) then make them proud
- Competitively engage with the competitor when they are relaxed
- When the competition appear united to the market place, separate, divide and split them and their activities
- Concentrate your market place activities where the competitor lacks preparation; and find markets & customers where the competitor would not expect you to find them

This is specialised approach to marketplace competition leads to victory and therefore all plans must be kept secret.

Before launching any marketplace competitive activity and in the confines of a place where one can reflect and contemplate, the leader must examine all of the previous considerations thoroughly.

The more thorough the considerations the greater the chances of winning in the marketplace. Less comprehensive considerations will lead to defeat.

Undertaking no considerations will lead to market forces dictating your success or failure, and you will not have control of your defeat or your victory. Your outcomes will not be of your doing. Defeat is probable.

> **❝** *To win one hundred victories in one hundred battles is not the acme of skill. To subdue the enemy without fighting is the acme of skill."*

Chapter Two
Marketplace Engagement

A robust method to get people, products and activity into the marketplace, and with equal capability to get people, products and processes out of the marketplace.

Generally then requirements of marketplace engagement are;

- The methods to include swift entrance and withdrawal capability with optimized mobility while in the marketplace arena.
- Have sufficient numbers of methods and tools available for the sales team to use while in the competitive marketplace.
- The means to achieve rapid distribution should early marketplace gains be won.
- The means to rapidly deploy further resources into the competitive marketplace.
- Methods to acknowledge submission or defeat, and/or methods to calculate the price of current marketplace protection.
- The ratio of engagement activity expenses to competitive marketplace personnel expenses must be set and closely managed.

Always seek quick gains when engaged in marketplace competitive engagements.

Long running marketplace competitive campaigns will reduce the effect of the tools and processes deployed. It will also reduce the energy, intensity and vigor of the execution.

Persistent and diligent blockades and/or attacks on the opposition's strong and easily defended position will weaken your staff to the point of mental exhaustion.

Corporate resources will become incompetent and incapable to deploy if staff are exposed to a prolonged campaign.

The competition will take advantage of these poor circumstances and then even the wisest of counsels will not be able to avert the consequences of such errors.

It is known that clumsy and swift campaigns yield greater results than skilled yet protracted campaigns.

No organization has ever gained from protracted campaigns in the competitive marketplace.

A complete knowledge of the benefits of competitive marketplace engagement can only be found by first understanding the inherent risks of such engagement.

In a competitive marketplace, benefits realized are directly proportional to risks known.

Those skilled at marketplace competition do not continue to apply resources on a number of occasions to achieve the same objective.

In the marketplace use Sales and Marketing tools developed by your organization. Take competitor's materials and supplies out of the hands of the competitor.

Then the sales force will have sufficient tools, materials and supplies.

An organization can be depleted of its resources if it continues to supply its sales force in the face of great obstacles.

Those inside the organization will become poorer should the organization ignore such obstacles.

Suppliers close to the sales force and the marketplace will supply tools and materials at higher than normal prices as they attempt to leverage their perceived strength.

The organization's wealth will be exhausted when the supply of tools and materials continues to be expensive.

When the wealth of the organization has been exhausted, all other employees will be asked to contribute more back to the organization.

When the strength of the sales force has been exhausted, the company's resources depleted, and all employees within the business are depleted, then 70% of the corporate wealth will be lost.

The organization's assets deployed in a continued prolonged marketplace competitive campaign will reach 60% of its reserves. Therefore a wise competitive leader will devote serious effort and/or energy to feed off the activities of the opposition.

Leveraging off the efforts of the competition will yield twenty fold results in either efficiencies or marketplace gains.

Destroying the competition will yield an adverse outcome over time.

Taking the competition's wealth is a matter of reward.

Therefore in the competitive marketplace, reward the first to capture multiple components of the competition's market share.

Once marketplace gains have been taken from the opposition, replace the opposition's processes and branding with your own.

Blend the captured market share with that which is yours and provided by you. Embrace opposition sales and marketing staff who join your organization.

This is known as defeating the competition, increasing your organization's market share, and your strength.

Therefore, it is important to seek victory in the competitive marketplace and not pursue a protracted, drawn-out competitive campaign.

Therefore, a leader who understands marketplace competitive processes and behaviors will be the custodian of the organization's people, and a respected leader in the stability of the organization.

> *In the practical art of war, the best thing of all is to take the enemy's country whole and intact; to shatter and destroy it is not so good.*"

Chapter Three
Planning Campaigns

Generally in the competitive marketplace, keeping the market in tact is best – destroying the market because of competition is inferior;

- Keeping the opposition's organization intact is best
  - destroying them as a consequence of marketplace competition is undistinguished.
- Keeping the opposition's sales & marketing operations intact is best
  - destroying the entire team is inferior.
- Keeping the opposition's sales force intact is best
  - destroying it is disappointing.
- Keeping the opposition's local sales team intact is best
  - destroying the local sales team is unsatisfactory.

Therefore, to win many times in many competitive marketplace battles is not the best outcome;

To bring under control and make submissive the opposition's sales & marketing operations and people without competing with them is the best outcome.

Therefore the best competitive strategy is to attack the opposition's plans, and then attack the opposition's alliances.

Only if these fail should you attack the opposition's organization; and only in the worst of cases attack a strong, impenetrable marketplace position that the opposition has gained. This must be the done only after all other options have been exhausted and/or are no longer available.

Attacking the opposition's organization will engage and consume substantial resources and an extended period of time.

In addition, the resources required to fortify and sustain the attack on the opposition's organization will undoubtedly extend the campaign for a further extended period of time.

If the leader of your sales force impetuously send the sales force into fight against the opposition's organization, then a very large percentage of them will leave your organization, and the opposition's organization will still be intact.

Expect this disastrous event to be marked by great loss and lasting distress and suffering.

Therefore, the leader who is skilled in competitive marketplace principles subdues the opposition without competing with them in the open marketplace, takes the competition's marketplace without open confrontation, and causes the downfall of the opposition quickly; and without a protracted open marketplace confrontation.

The leader's aim is to take the entire marketplace and to keep it intact. Therefore, your competitive tools will remain in good condition, and marketplace gains will be intact.

These are the principles of planning marketplace competition.

Generally in marketplace competition;

- Surround and prepare to capture the opposition's market share if your sales force's capability is substantially greater than that of the opposition.
- Undertake direct marketplace competition if your sales force's capability is significantly better than that of the opposition.
- Divide the competition's marketplace presence if your sales force's capability is known to be better than that of the opposition.
- Ensure your sales force's capability to compete if your sales force's capability is equal to that of the opposition.
- Be able to evade the competition if your sales force's capability is less than that of the opposition.
- Be able to avoid the competition if your sales force's capability is much less than that of the opposition.

Therefore, a smaller competitive organization's marketplace presence that is inflexible will be captured by larger competitive organizations.

The competitive leader is the custodian of the organization.

The competitive organization will certainly be strong when the competitive leader upholds, defends and promotes its organization and its activities. Without this support, the competitive organization will certainly be weakened.

There are three issues the competitive leader must avoid.

- Firstly; attempting to move forward into a competitive marketplace when the organization is in no position to advance, and attempting to pull back from a competitive position when the organization is in no position to withdraw. This can be a perplexing, troublesome situation that will become complicated.
- Secondly; managing the sales team as if there is no competition will confuse them.
- Thirdly; a competitive leader who exercises control while not knowing the competitive marketplace will make the organization hesitant.

When the competitive organization is confused and hesitant, other competitive organizations will take advantage of the situation and will win market share.

Therefore, there are five factors a competitive organization must know to win in the competitive marketplace.

- To win in the competitive marketplace an organization must know when it is able and capable of competing; and when it is not.
- To win in the competitive marketplace, an organization must know how to use both large and small measures of competitive activities.
- To win in the competitive marketplace, an organization must have a unifying united purpose that permeates the entire organization.
- To win in the competitive marketplace, an organization must be prepared to wait for the unprepared.
- To win in the competitive marketplace, non-competitive organizational staff must not interfere with a capable and competent competitive leader.

These five factors will predict who will win in the competitive marketplace.

Therefore Sun Tzu says:

- A leader who knows the organization's and the opposition's capabilities, strengths, weaknesses, opportunities, threats, and their activities will survive many competitive engagements.
- A leader who knows the organization's capabilities, strengths, weaknesses, opportunities, threats and activities, but does not know that of the opposition, will sometimes win and sometimes lose competitive engagements.
- A leader who knows the opposition's capabilities, strengths, weaknesses, opportunities, threats and activities, but is less familiar with that of his/her own organization, will be at considerable risk with every competitive engagement.

> **❝** *The good fighters of old first put themselves beyond the possibility of defeat, and then waited for an opportunity of defeating the enemy."*

Chapter Four
Resource Formation

Those skilled in competitive marketplace engagement make themselves invincible and then wait for the opposition to become vulnerable.

An organization being invincible depends on the organization; but the opposition becoming vulnerable depends on the opposition. Therefore, those skilled in competitive marketplace engagements can make themselves invincible, but cannot necessarily cause the opposition to become vulnerable.

Therefore it is said that an organization may know how to win in the competitive marketplace but cannot necessarily accomplish such victories.

- An organization adopts a position of invincibility while defending, and adopts a position of vulnerability while competing.
- An organization adopts a position of competency while defending, and adopts a position of inadequacy while attacking.
- Organizations skilled in defence conceal themselves in the most fortified position available. Organizations skilled in competitive engagement position themselves in a variety of positions in the marketplace.

Organizations that consider and adopt these various positions, protect themselves and are better able to achieve in the marketplace gains.

Awareness of a marketplace gain where everyone becomes aware is not the best outcome.

Winning competitive marketplace engagements such that everyone says "excellent" is not the best outcome.

Raising something that is in decline is not considered a strength. Seeing such large objects as the sun and moon is not considered to possessing sharp vision. Hearing thunder is not considered a sign of sensitive hearing.

In ancient times, those who are skilled in competition gained victory where victory was easily gained. Therefore, those organizations that win in the competitive marketplace do so because there has not been any miscalculations or poor considerations prior to or during competitive marketplace engagements.

Wisdom and courage alone do not guarantee marketplace gains.

Miscalculations and/or poor marketplace considerations will lead to eventual losses in competitive marketplace engagements.

No miscalculations will provide greater certainty in competitive marketplace engagements; winning market share from those who have already lost through miscalculation and/or poor considerations.

Therefore, those skilled in competitive marketplace engagements establish market positions that make them invincible. They do not miss opportunities to attack the opposition.

Therefore, the organization that wins competitive marketplace engagements must first obtain the conditions to win; and then seeks to engage the opposition in marketplace battles.

- Organizations that seek to engage the opposition in marketplace battles before first obtaining the conditions in which to win, will lose.

- Organizations skilled in the marketplace cultivate organizational alignment and preserve executional efficiency and effectiveness in the marketplace. Such organizations experience successful competitive marketplace engagements, choosing when to win or when to strategically relinquish a position.

The factors in competitive marketplace engagements are:

First: Measurement

Measurements are deduced from competitive positioning in the arena of the market place and the operational risks associated with engagements.

Second: Quantity

Quantities are deduced from Measurements.

Third: Calculation

Calculations are deduced from Quantities.

Fourth: Comparison

Comparisons are deduced from Calculations.

Fifth: Victory

Victories are deduced from Comparisons.
And Victories are marketplace gains from competitive engagements.

An organization that has marketplace gains from competitive engagements is an enormously powerful and strong entity.

An organization that loses market share from competitive engagements is considerably weakened and vulnerable.

The enormous power and strength gained from such engagements provides considerable momentum for an organization to carve out its marketplace position.

This is formation.

" Confront them with annihilation, and they will then survive; plunge them into a deadly situation, and they will then live. When people fall into danger, they are then able to strive for victory."

Chapter Five
Force

Generally, leading many people is similar in nature to leading a few. It is a matter of dividing the competitive organization into groups.

Undertaking competitive marketplace engagements with the resources of a large organization is similar to undertaking competitive marketplace engagements with the resources of a small organization.

Efficient and reliable communications is the key.

Common and uncommon actions taken to gain a tactical end through skilful and clever management of affairs will enable an organization to successfully engage marketplace competitors.

The strength of the organization will easily destroy the fragility of the competition. It is a matter of weaknesses and strength.

Generally, in competitive marketplace engagements, use common maneuvers to engage the competitor, and uncommon maneuvers to win market share from the competitor.

There are a large inexhaustible number of competitive leaders skilled at uncommon actions taken to gain a tactical end through skilful and clever management of affairs.

Such competitive leaders are both apparent and difficult to find, but nonetheless are predictably there.

Such competitive leaders shine, rest, hibernate, and rejuvenate.

There are many examples where a number of variations are derived from the base, yet not all possibilities are known.

In competitive marketplace engagements, there is only two types of proactive, preemptive campaigns to gain market share;

Uncommon and common – yet all of the variations of both approaches cannot be comprehended.

Uncommon and common approaches feed into each other, compliment each other, operate in a synergistic manner, and in a continuous cycle.

It is impossible to comprehend all of the possibilities and variations along with the countless interactions.

The rush of torrential waters tossing boulders illustrates force. The strike of a bird of prey breaking the body of its target illustrates timing.

Therefore, the force of those skilled in competitive marketplace engagements is overwhelming, and their timing precise.

Their force is like a drawn crossbow and their timing is like the release of the trigger.

A sales team with such force and timing capabilities will not be confused in the competitive marketplace, even when the competitive behaviors of the market seem chaotic.

- A sales team with such force and timing capabilities will not be defeated in the competitive marketplace, even when it appears as if they are not progressing.
- Order, courage and strength gives rise to and commands disorder, fear and weakness in the competitive marketplace.
- Disorder is correlated to disorganization. Fear is derived from a lack of understanding of force. Weakness is derived from poor formation.
- Those skilled in positioning and manipulating the opposition use the techniques of formation in such a way that the opposition must respond.
- Your organization tempts the competitor with marketplace offers that manipulate the competitor into changing its position and allowing your organization to ambush and out manoeuvre them.

Companies skilled in competitive marketplace engagements aim to gain market share through the use of force having little requirements for individual effort.

Therefore, the skilled competitive marketplace leader will select the right people for each campaign who are able to exploit force.

The competitive marketplace leader who can exploit force is able to easily lead the sales team who in turn gather momentum.

A stable marketplace will allow the sales team to remain still. A marketplace that is dynamic, changing and moving will engage the momentum of the sales team.

But even with a dynamic, changing and moving marketplace, a sales team that does not have the capability to generate momentum will remain still.

Therefore, those skilled in competitive marketplace engagements who use force where the sales team is engaged in a campaign, have momentum.

This is force.

> **"** *Whoever is first in the field and awaits the coming of the enemy, will be fresh for the fight; whoever is second in the field and has to hasten to battle will arrive exhausted."*

Chapter Six
Weakness & Strength

Generally, the first to occupy a market is comfortable.

The competitor who comes into an occupied market will be stretched, tested, and will require a sustained effort.

Therefore, those skilled at competitive market place engagements can position the opposition in the market, and will not themselves be positioned by the opposition.

Allowing the opposition to enter a market acknowledges the advantage(s) of the opposition.

Preventing the opposition from entering a market means that punitive consequences of doing so must be demonstrated or inflicted.

- Therefore, if the opposition is comfortable in the market, be able to consume their resources.
- If the opposition has plenty of resources, deprive them of future resources.
- If the opposition is in a desired position in the market place, be able to move them to another segment, or out.

Give the opposition the impression they have a market presence that they must defend. Get to market segments fast where the opposition least expects you to be.

Your business can easily occupy market segments where the opposition has no tangible presence.

Be certain to own the market segment you occupy. Go after markets where the opposition cannot defend its position.

To ensure the safety of your position; only defend a market position where the opposition cannot attack.

Therefore, the opposition will not know how to defend their market presence against those who are well experienced in entering new market segments.

The opposition will not know how to enter a market segment against those who are well experienced in defending their market presence.

Being subtle in market place engagements will make you appear to be without order or structure.

Appearing to be confused or puzzled in the market place will make you appear to be unfathomable.

Therefore those who are able to master the art of subtly while being unfathomable will dictate the outcomes of the competition in the marketplace.

- To achieve marketplace gains, move swiftly to the opposition's weak points.
- Possess marketplace agility and move with superior speed to a position that cannot be pursued by the opposition.

Therefore, if you choose to compete, even if the competition is strong, they will be drawn into the competitive market you create because they must protect what you go after.

If you choose not to compete, even if you choose simply to define your competitive boundaries, the opposition will not compete, because their movements will be diverted to protect what they have.

Therefore, if you can get the competition to show their position while you appear to be without order or structure, you will be at full force while the opposition is divided.

If your business is operating at full capacity and the opposition is divided, then the competitive forces of your attacks on the opposition will seem incredible and overwhelming.

Therefore, your business will have a broader market presence and the competitor's presence will be sparse.

- If you compete with your organization's full capacity against the competitors' depleted and divided presence, then the competitor will be in dire straits.
- The competitor must not know where your organization is going to compete. If it is kept secret, the competitor must be prepared to defend in many places.
- If the competitor is forced to mount a defensive strategy across many market place fronts, then their presence and capacity to execute will be marginalised.

Therefore, if the competitor prepares to defend in a sector of the market, other sectors possessed by the competitor will be exposed.

If the competitor prepares to defend across many market place fronts, then every sector the opposition currently holds will be exposed.

There are few who actually prepare to defend against competitor's proactive marketplace activities. There are many who will want others to do the work necessary to defend against such competitor activities.

- Therefore, if you know when and where you want to engage in the market, you will be able to organise your resources to compete.

- If you do not know when and where you want to engage in the market, then different and complimentary parts of your organization cannot provide support to each other during any ensuing competitive activity.

There will be even less support if your organization becomes distracted, disjointed and uncoordinated by other activities.

Based on Sun Tzu's calculations,

though the opposition may have many resources, if they do not understand their strengths and weaknesses, they will not gain in the competitive market place.

Therefore Sun Tzu says

that winning can be achieved if you understand your strengths and weaknesses.

Though the competitor may have many resources, they can be excluded from the competitive market place.

Therefore, understand the competitor's market plans and understand how they will use their strengths to achieve their goals. Also know their weakness so that you can exploit them.

- Provoke your competitors so that you may understand their responses.
- Understand your competitors position in the market so that you know where they generate revenue and where they can lose revenue.
- Probe your competitor to understand their strengths and weaknesses.

The ultimate superior outcome is to take a market position where you appear to be without order or structure.

- If you appear to be without order or structure, the most penetrating examination of your business by the opposition will not be able to detect or recognise your activities. The smartest people will not be able to work out what you are capable of doing, or how you will execute your plans.
- If you appear to be without order or structure to the competitors, your own sales and marketing team will not fully comprehend how market place gains were won.
- People may know how you prepared your business to win in the market place, yet no one will know the activities, resources and methods that were used to create market place gains.

Therefore, strategies to gain in the market place are not to be repetitious, and the variety of resources, methods and activities deployed are to be endless.

The structure of market place execution is to be adaptable with a high degree of mobility.

Successful market place execution avoids strong competitive activities, but moves swiftly to take advantage of weak, exposed opportunities.

The sales team must be highly adaptable, flexible and mobile so as to effectively deal with any opposition activity and to make market place gains.

Therefore, the sales team must not be well structured and not have a predictable presence.

Those sales team's that are able to adapt and change in accord with the competitors and achieve market place gains through Sun Tzu's wisdom are the best asset any organization can have.

Therefore, there are never any constants in the competitive market place. There is never a predictable set of circumstances.

> *Strategy without tactics is the slowest route to victory. Tactics without strategy is the noise before defeat."*

Chapter Seven
Competitive Activity

Generally, the principles of competitive activity are:

The leader of sales and marketing will obtain the corporate sales & marketing strategy from the company's strategic plan. The resources needed to achieve the goals of the plan are obtained and made operationally ready to execute. Operational head quarters is established.

There is nothing more difficult than competitive market place engagement.

In the competitive market place, it is difficult to turn the winding course into a direct path to market, and in turning adversity into advantages.

Therefore if your team is able make the competitor's route to market a winding course, and manipulate their activities so they believe that they are taking an advantageous path to market, though you may seem behind your competitor, you will engage the market faster.

You must know both the winding path to market, and the most direct path to market to win competitive market place engagements.

Therefore, competitive activity has advantages, but has risks.

- If the entire sales team is mobilized to take advantage of an opportunity, then you will not be first to market.

- If a portion of the sales team mobilizes to take advantage of an opportunity, then your resources will be lost.

For these reasons, if you move too quickly to take advantage of a market opportunity, committing too many resources too quickly and for too long a period, then a significant part of your market will be lost.

- The strongest of your sales team will take advantage of a market opportunity quickly, and as a rule, only a small percentage (perhaps 10%) will actually be in an position to take advantageous steps. The rest of your sales team will need to catch up.
- If your business struggles to take up an advantageous position distant from your current position, then the competitive leader's efforts will be thwarted. The amount of loss endured in a struggle for an advantageous market position is directly proportional to the distance, or how far your current market is away from that new market position.

For these reasons, a sales team without the necessary sales execution tools will fail.

If the sales team is without means to undertake competitive activities, it will fail.

If the sales team has limited or no resource reserves, it will fail in competitive engagements.

Therefore, a competitive leader who does not understand the intentions of non-competitive market place participants will be unable to secure alliances.

If the competitive leader does not know or understand the competitive market landscape that the sales team must traverse, then the sales team cannot move forward to win new markets.

The competitive leader who does not use local market place intelligence cannot take advantage of the competitive positioning in the arena of the market place and the operational risks associated with engagement.

Therefore, the sales team is established on deception, mobilized by advantage, and changed through dividing up and consolidating the sales team.

Therefore, the sales team advances with ease and where it chooses to.

- The sales team advances with unstoppable strength.
- The sales team moves into and takes new markets with force.
- The sales team is firm in its position.
- The sales team appears as if it is nowhere, but is everywhere.
- The sales team strikes with enormous power and focus.

Make sure that the sales team is rewarded proportional to the markets won.

Having won a market, divide it and hold advantageous segments.

Consolidate, contemplate and understand your new market position; then move on to the next competitive market opportunity.

The competitive leader who knows the winding course and a direct path to market will win competitive markets.

This is competitive market dynamics.

The doctrine of competitive engagement operations says:

- It's because normal communications can be distorted during competitive engagements that other more reliable means of communications are to be established.
- It's because the sales team may be unable to know exactly where each other is that identifiable but secret means of communications must be established.

When the sales team is united, the stronger team members will not gain markets alone, and the slower support team members wont return to headquarters alone.

Therefore, during competitive engagements where it is difficult to communicate, the use of reliable communications not capable of distortion must be deployed. Engage secret communication methods when the competitor can observe your activities.

Use a means of communication that is capable of unified messaging. Ensure the emotional intensity of communications unites the sales team's hearts and minds.

These are the principles for employing a large sales team.

- The energy of the sales team can be dampened and the competitive leader's mind can be dampened.
- Therefore, at the beginning of a competitive engagement, energy is high but will decline during the process only to be exhausted by the end of the engagement.
- Therefore, those skilled in the use of force avoid engaging the competitor at beginning of the marketing campaign, and instead make their moves when the competitor's energy is exhausted at the end of the campaign.

This is the way to manage energy.

- If the competitor is disciplined, wait for disorder.
- If the competitor is calm, wait for clamor.

This is the way to manage the mind.

- If the competitor is close to your desired marketplace, then you should wait for there to be some apparent distance between them and the market. Wait for your sales team to be close and united.
- If the competitor appears to have capability and ready to go, then you should wait for them to appear fatigued. Wait for those in your sales team to be at full readiness.

- If the competitor has many resources, then you should wait for those resources to be depleted. Ensure your resources are optimal.

This is the way to manage strength.

- Do not engage the competitor with obvious organization or with well regulated operational activity.

This is the way to manage adaptation.

Therefore, the principles of competitive engagement are:

- Do not engage a competitor who has a strong market presence, or is in a 'must survive' position in the market with no other market options.
- Do not pursue a false withdrawal from the market staged by the competitor.
- Do not competitively engage the competitor who has known and vastly superior sales and marketing capabilities.
- Do not be lured into falsely constructed situations.
- Do not defeat the hopes and aspirations of a competitor who is withdrawing from the market.
- If you do gain a new market that was occupied by the competitor, be sure to provide a dignified exit for them.
- Do not put undue pressure on a competitor that has no other option but to leave the market you have gained.

These are the principles of competitive marketplace engagement.

" *He who knows when he can fight and when he cannot, will be victorious."*

Chapter Eight
Ten Variables

Generally, the principles of competitive marketplace engagement are:

The competitive leader will obtain the corporate sales & marketing strategy from the company's strategic plan. The resources needed to achieve the goals of the plan are obtained and made operationally ready to execute.

- Do not establish competitive headquarters in positions that are difficult to manage.
- Unite non-competing marketplace participants where markets have a synergistic intersection.
- Do not remain in one position in the open marketplace.
- Ensure your sales team is always ready to engage when in a marketplace that has many potential competitors.
- Engage the competitor in markets where there can be only one major/preferred provider of goods and/or services.
- There are approaches to markets not to be taken.
- There are competitors that should not be engaged.
- There are strongly held markets that should not be pursued and competitively engaged.
- There are markets that should not be entered.
- There are sales execution tactics and objectives that should be ignored.

Therefore, the competitive leader who knows the advantages of these ten variables knows how to utilise the sales team's efforts to the best advantage.

If the competitive leader does not know the advantages of the ten variables, then even with good marketplace intelligence, the competitive leader will not be able to take advantage of the marketplace.

The competitive leader who does not know the principles of the ten variables but understands five advantages will not be able to optimize the sales force's activities.

Therefore the intelligent competitive leader contemplates both the advantages and disadvantages of the ten variables.

- The competitive leader can complete comprehensive considerations by contemplating the advantages.
- The competitive leader can remove difficulties and barriers by contemplating the disadvantages.

Therefore, defeat the competitive market place participants with potential disadvantages, labour the competitive market place participants with constant matters, and have competitive market place participants rush after advantages.

So the principles of competitive marketplace engagement are:

- Do not rely on the competitor to enter your market or for the competitor to defend against your entry to the market, but rely on your sales team's readiness to engage with the competitor.
- Do not rely on the competitor to not defend its position in the marketplace, but rely on your strong market position being able to withstand competition.

Therefore, there are five dangerous traits of a competitive leader;

- The competitive leader that is reckless can lose whole markets.
- The competitive leader that is fearful, hesitant and afraid will lose control.
- The competitive leader that is quick tempered will be easily insulted.
- The competitive leader that is overly principled can be easily embarrassed.
- The competitive leader that is overly concerned with individuals within the sales team can be overly worried and cautious.

These five traits are faults in a competitive leader, and are disastrous in competitive marketplace engagements.

The sales team's demise and the loss of a competitive leader are due to these five dangerous traits.

They must be examined.

Chapter Nine
Sales Team Maneuvers

Generally, on positioning the sales team and observing the competitor:

- To get to markets that are difficult to reach, choose an approach that requires the least effort to enter it.
- Observe the competitor from an overall perspective and with clarity, such that is difficult for you to be observed.
- If the competitor holds a strong market position, do not send your sales team into a competitive engagement.

This is positioning the sales team in a strong market position.

- After the sales team has negotiated barriers to marketplace entry, they must not revisit those barriers or the issues associated with them. Leave no evidence of your sales team's ability to deal with those barriers.
- If the competitor attempts to negotiate marketplace entry barriers, do not undertake competitive engagements while the competitor is dealing with those barriers.
- When it appears that half of the competitor's sales team has passed through the barriers to marketplace entry, it will then be advantageous to competitively engage.
- If you decide to engage the competitor, do not allow your sales team to undertake activities before the competitor has commenced to negotiate the barriers to marketplace entry.

- Make sure you take an overall perspective of the marketplace observing with clarity and difficult for the competitor to observe, and do not allow your sales team to be anywhere near the barriers to marketplace entry.

This is the approach the sales team must take with barriers to marketplace entry.

- Once your sales team has successfully negotiated marketplace barriers to entry, move them quickly to the market.
- If the sales team is competitively engaged while themselves negotiating barriers to marketplace entry, then conceal their activities and provide a defensive resting place.

This is positioning the sales team while dealing with barriers to marketplace entry.

In an open competitive market, position your sales team such that it is easy for them to move to a variety of competitive or defensive positions. They should be able to clearly see the overall operations of the market, know the competitive landscape, and know where the defensive position is.

This is positioning the sales team in an open competitive market.

These are the four positions advantageous to the sales team, which will enable them to capture many markets.

- the sales team prefers to clearly see the overall operations of the market, values clarity and avoids ambiguity
- avoids being observed by the competition
- has sufficient resources and capabilities
- is in a constant state of readiness

These factors mean certainty in gaining positions in markets.

Ensure the sales team always has clarity wherever there are obstacles or market niches or barriers or advantages, and ensure a strong defensive position.

These are the advantages to the sales team.

- Use the competitive positioning in the arena of the market place and the operational risks associated with engagement to your advantage.
- Where an operational risk seems likely, wait until it manifests itself and allow the market to deal with it; then allow your sales team to move to the market.
- When the competitive positioning in the arena of the market place and the operational risks associated with engagement seem insurmountable, then you must quickly move your sales team away from that marketplace.
- Do not attempt to embrace such a competitive and risky marketplace.
- When there is sufficient distance between your sales team and the competitive risky market, draw the competition to this competitive risky market.
- When your sales team engages with the competition they will already be heavily involved with operational risks and a competitive marketplace.
- When the sales force is significantly engaged in a marketplace that is characterized by opportunistic positions, be careful of opposition intelligence gatherers as there will be many opportunities for them to be unrecognizable.
- If the competitor occupies a market space close to your own and appears to be docile, they are occupying a naturally strong position.
- If the competitor occupies a market space that seems distant and unlike the one you occupy, then the competitor wants to engage with you in open competition, because the competitor occupies a clear market position that is to their advantage.

❝ If you know the enemy and know yourself you need not fear the results of a hundred battles."

Chapter Ten
Market Formation

The competitive positioning in the arena of the market place and the operational risks associated with engagement can be characterized as accessible, entrapping, no-win, narrow, difficult, or expansive.

- If your sales team can enter the market arena but the competitor cannot, then this is called an accessible market.

  For an accessible market arena, first gain a clear perspective of the market, and what the most convenient methods are to maintain market penetration. You can then compete with the advantage.

- If you are able to enter the market but find it difficult to withdraw, then it is called entrapping.

  For an entrapping market arena, if the competitor is unprepared for marketplace entry, then competitively engage them to win market share.

If the competition is prepared for marketplace entry and you attempt to engage them competitively and do not gain market share and do not win market share, then it will be difficult to withdraw. This is disadvantageous.

If there are no advantages for either your sales team or the competitor to enter into a market, then this is a no-win market.

- In a no-win market, if the competitor's activity or inactivity lead to what seems to be a marketplace opportunity, then dismiss it and walk away. Withdraw your sales team.

  When it appears that half of the competitor's sales team has entered a no-win marketplace, it will then be advantageous to competitively engage.

- In a narrow, tight market, your sales team must occupy it first; Your sales team must be prepared to compete, and patiently wait for the competitor.
  If the competitor occupies a narrow tight market first, and has capability to engage your sales team and compete, do not enter this market.
  If the competitor is not able to compete, then enter the market and engage them competitively.

- For markets difficult to access, if you occupy it first, have a market presence that provides your sales team with overall clarity and a position difficult for the competitor to observe your activities; and wait for the competitor.
  If the competitor occupies markets that are difficult to access, then do not attempt to enter it; withdraw from that market.

- For an open expansive market, if your sales team's capabilities are the same as the competitor's, it will be difficult to engage competitively. There is no advantage in competitive engagements in such a market.

These are the six Ways to approach the market. They are the leader's responsibility and must be thoroughly understood and considered.

In competitive marketplace engagements, there are situations of undisciplined, insubordination, deterioration, collapse, chaos, and setback.

These six situations are not caused by the changing ebbs and flows of markets, or the competitive positioning in the market place & the operational risks associated with engagement – but by the leader.

1   If the competition's capabilities are equal to yours and a part of your sales team engages on many competitive fronts, then this is called undisciplined.

2   If the sales team is strong but their immediate and most direct supervisor/leaders are weak, this will lead to insubordination.

3   If the most direct supervisor/leaders are strong but the sales team is weak, then this will lead to deterioration.

4   If the sales team's most direct supervisor/leaders are angry and insubordinate, undertaking competitive marketplace engagements with such a disposition, and the senior leader does not know of their abilities, this will lead to collapse.

5   If the senior leader is weak and not disciplined, and unable to give clear directions, the entire sales effort lacks discipline and their positions in the market are in disarray, then this is called chaos.

6   If the leader cannot understand and contemplate the competitor, and deploys limited resources when great capacity is needed, less capable or competing against a more capable opposition, and has no selected forward market engagement activities and/ or positions, this is called setback.

These are the six Ways of defeat. They are the leader's responsibility, and must be carefully and thoroughly understood & considered.

Competitive positioning in the market place arena and knowing the operational risks associated with engagement assist the sales team.

To understand the competition, create conditions that lead to gaining market share; determining the risks and resources required to do so. They are the Ways of the superior leader.

The sales teams and leaders who engage competitively and know these factors are certain to gain market share.

The sales teams and leaders who engage competitively and do not know these factors are certain to lose market share.

Therefore, if the Way of competitive market place engagements indicates certain market share gains, though the company does not want to engage competitively, the leader may compete.

If the Way of competitive market place engagements indicates market share loss, though the company wants to compete, the leader may not compete.

Therefore, the leader who does not engage competitively to seek glory, or does not withdraw from market opportunities to avoid ridicule, but cares for only the company's security and promotes the company's interest, is acting in the shareholder's interests.

- The leader sees the sales team as an intricate part of the company's health and well being; and they will strive to achieve marketplace gains in the toughest markets.
- The leader sees the sales team as a fundamental part of a singular overall corporate team; and they will support the leader against all odds.

- If the leader is too soft on the sales team, and cannot deploy them; or if the leader is too personally engaged with the sales team, and cannot give directions; or if the leader does not discipline the sales team, and cannot establish clear account-abilities; then the sales team will behave liked spoiled children and be useless.
- If the leader knows the sales team can competitively engage, but does not know the competitor is unable to engage, then the market share gain is incomplete.
- If the leader knows the competitor can be competitively engaged, but does not know the sales team is unable to engage, then the market share gain is incomplete.
- If the leader knows the competitor can be competitively engaged, and knows the sales team can engage, but does not understand the market place, then the market share gain is incomplete.

Therefore, the leader who knows how to competitively engage the sales team is limitless when executing tactical moves.

Therefore I say, if the leader knows the competition's capabilities and readiness, and knows the sales team capabilities and readiness, then market share gain is not at risk.

If the leader knows the absolutes of competition, the slow market pace and fast market place, the changing ebbs and flows of the markets, the competitive positioning in the arena of the market place, and the operational risks associated with engagement; then market share gain is assured.

> **"** *The opportunity to secure ourselves against defeat lies in our own hands, but the opportunity of defeating the enemy is provided by the enemy himself."*

Chapter Eleven
9 Market Engagement Risks

The principles of competitive marketplace engagements (or Grounds) are:

1 Dispersive Ground

Where a business engages competitively in their own markets, this is called a dispersive Ground; where markets can be broken up.

2 Marginal Ground

When a business enters another's business's market, with minimal penetration, this is called a marginal Ground.

3 Contentious Ground

Where it is advantageous for both your business and your competition to occupy a market, then this is called a contentious Ground.

4 Open Ground

Where there is no market barriers, restrictions or impedances to either your company or any competitors, this is called open Ground.

5 Intersecting Ground

Where the market is closely watched and scrutinized by all possible competitive participants, and the first business to reach that market will enjoy the support of that market; this is called intersecting Ground.

6 Critical Ground

Where a business deeply penetrates a competitor's market, where the competitor has a strong hold on that market, and the penetrating business can only move further into that market, this is called critical Ground.

7 Difficult Ground

Where there are many difficulties, barriers, impediments, and unclear paths to markets, this is called difficult Ground.

8 Surrounded Ground

Where the path to market is narrowly defined, the path from that market is ambiguous and unclear, allowing the competition to competitively engage your sales team using minimal resources, this is called surrounded Ground.

9 Deadly Ground

Where if a business engages competitively deploying all resources and gains critical market share, and a business who does not engage competitively deploying all resources and loses critical market share; this is called deadly Ground.

Therefore,

- On dispersive Ground - do not engage competitively.
- On marginal Ground - do not stop.
- On contentious Ground - do not engage competitively.
- On open Ground - do not allow your sales team to be disaggregated and/or dispersed.
- On intersecting Ground - form alliances with non- competing market participants.
- On critical Ground - launch an aggressive market campaign as an all-out assault to gain market share.
- On difficult Ground - continue the pursuit to achieve market share.
- On surrounded Ground - ensure your sales team is capable and ready to engage competitively.
- On deadly Ground - engage competitively.

In times gone by, those skilled at competitive market place engagements were able to prevent the unity of the competition's sales team; prevent the unity of the many and of the few; prevent the unity of the workers and the business owners; and the unity of the competition's leaders and the employees who work in and support that business.

Ensure the competitor's sales team is separated, dis-aggregated, dispersed and unable to quickly consolidate.

Should the competitor's resources be in a consolidated position, then ensure they are not organized.

Mobilise your sales team when it is advantageous to do so, and ensure they hold positions when it is not advantageous to move forward into markets.

Ask:

If the competition has great capability, mobility and strength, and moves into a market place, what should be the response?

Sun Tzu says:

Take whatever part of the market place the competitor values most, and then they will respond to your business's every request.

The essential factors in competitive market place engagements are mobility, speed, and agility.

To take advantage of the competition's lack of readiness, take unexpected approaches to competitively engage them in market place where the competition is unprepared.

Generally, the Way of moving swiftly into the competition's market place is when your sales team has already achieved deep market penetration, and the sales team is united.

The competition will not be able to win back the market share lost to your sales team.

If your sales team aggressively gains market share in a fruitful, profitable market, then the sales team will have plenty of resources.

If you take care of the health of your sales team, avoid working them too hard, they will be united, and will build strength.

When executing sales tactical moves and contemplating sales strategy, be flexible in your thoughts on order.

Manoeuvre the sales team into situations where there is no escape from the full competitive might of the competitors, where they will lose market share, lose their jobs, before the competitor's assault is over.

When your sales team is in dire straits, what can they not do? They will exert their full strength and ingenuity.

When the sales team is in desperate situations, they will fear nothing.

Having penetrated deep into the competitor's strongly held market place, they will be united.

When there are no other alternatives, the sales team will fight.

Therefore,

- Though not disciplined, the sales team remain alert.
- Though not asked, the sales team are committed.
- Though without promises, the sales team are loyal to the business.
- And though the sales team is not managed tightly, they are trustworthy.

Prohibit prophecies of future events, and get rid of doubts, and they will vanish without any other thought.

The sales team may not have wealth, but not because they dislike material goods.

Members of the sales team do not remain with one company, but not because the dislike long time service.

On the day the sales team are given specific objectives to competitively engage in the market place, there will be a variety of emotions from willingness to refusal.

However, if they are put into a desperate market place situation, they will have legendary courage.

Those skilled in warfare are like a serpent.

Always ready to strike when the opportunity presents itself. And they strike with precision and lethality using its head, its tail, or both at once.

The leader knows that the world is filled with dichotomies and that for every action there is an equal and opposite reaction. The leader will always try to create options that will produce advantages.

The leader needs to be able to tell when advantages are exploitable and when they are potential traps.

During conflict observe the competitor's market place position. Decipher whether they have overlooked a possible opening in their defences.

Once it is known, your sales team must not hesitate to take advantage before the competitor recognizes their mistake.

Ask:

Can forces be made like the serpent?

Sun Tzu says: They can.

When two competing forces are both exposed to the same adverse conditions, they will assist each other in order for each of them to survive; like left and right hands.

Therefore, containing and reducing the competition's capability is not enough.

The Way of organization is uniting the sales team's emotional energy, and optimizing the balance between the strong and the weak through the principles of the Ground (competitive market place positioning and operational risks associated with engagements).

Therefore, one skilled in competitive market place engagements personally leads the entire sales and marketing effort, as if they, the whole team, is one person.

The sales team then cannot but follow.

> ❝ *Invincibility lies in the defence; the possibility of victory in the attack.*"

Chapter Twelve
Disruptive Attacks

Sun Tzu speaks of fire attacks in a military sense; which are viewed as disruptive attacks in the market place. Proper deployment can make the difference between effectual and ineffectual, and improper deployment can be harmful. One must factor in the motions of the forces at work behind such strategies to calculate the effect of such a strategy.

There are five kinds of disruptive attacks:

1 disrupting personnel;

2 disrupting resources;

3 disrupting equipment;

4 disrupting resource storage facilities;

5 disrupting competitive sales & marketing tools.

Using disruptive attacks depends on appropriate conditions. Resources required to undertake disruptive attacks must be available before commencement of such activities.

There are appropriate times in the marketing and sales cycles for using disruptive attacks, and appropriate conditions when to commence such an attack.

The appropriate time in the cycles is when the market is rich with needs and frustrations emanating from sub-standard supplier activities to the market.

The appropriate conditions are when the competition is unaware that your efforts will manifest in the most influential way.

The market will provide you with indicators that a disruptive attack is needed to correct the inadequacies present.

Generally, in disruptive attacks, you must respond according to the five variables in the disruptive nature of the attacks.

- If the disruptive attacks are initiated inside the competitors market and/or headquarters, your sales team must respond quickly outside of the competitors market and/or headquarters.
- If the disruptive attacks are initiated and the competitor remains unperturbed, then wait, do not undertake competitive market place engagements.
- Let the disruption reach its optimum point, and follow up if you can; stay out of the disrupted market place if you can.
- If the disruptive attack can be initiated from outside the target marketplace without relying on being in that market place, then initiate the disruption when the time is right.
- If the disruption moves away from the competitor, do not engage the competitor away from the disruption.

There will be a time when marketplace activities will be steady enough to optimize the initiation of a disruptive attack.

Your sales team must know the five variables of disruption, to be able to understand the optimal disruptive timing.

Those who use disruptive methods to assist in attacks are intelligent; those who use elimination methods to assist in attacks are powerful.

Elimination methods can be used to prevent the competition from engaging in a market, but cannot be used to forcibly disrupt the competition.

If your sales team gain market share in a competitive engagement and is successful in disruptive attacks and/or elimination methods, but does not exploit those achievements, it is disastrous.

This is called waste and delay.

Therefore Sun Tzu says, the wise leader thinks about it, and the good leader executes it.

- If it is not advantageous, do not advance into a market.
- If there is no gain, do not deploy your sales teams.
- If there are no market place risks, do not competitively engage.
- The business must not deploy the sales team out of anger.
- The leader must not engage competitively out of wrath.
- If it is advantageous, deploy your sales team and advance into a market.
- If it is not advantageous, do not do not deploy resources and do not advance into a market.

Those who are angry will be happy again, and those wrathful will be cheerful again, but a destroyed market place cannot exist again; a destroyed market cannot be returned to its previous state.

Therefore, the enlightened business is prudent, and the good leader is cautious.

This is the Way of securing your business and its place in a market; and preserving the sales and marketing teams.

" If ignorant both of your enemy and yourself, you are certain to be in peril."

Chapter Thirteen
Using Intelligence Providers

Generally, deploying large sales teams towards not easy to get to markets, will result in very large expenses and a depletion of the business's resources.

Those who are agitated and unsettled, those who have laboured long and hard, and those who are unable to undertake normal daily work, will be many when such a large sales team deployment takes place.

Two competitors may have a counter balancing effect in a marketplace for quite a long period, so as to be ready to engage competitively to decisively win market share on a specific occasion.

Yet one refusing to deploy resources to learn of the competitor's situation is the height of ignorance.

This is not the leader of people, an aid to the business, or the expert who can gain market share.

What enables enlightened businesses and good leaders to gain market share and beat the competition at every move and to be extraordinarily successful is foreknowledge.

Foreknowledge cannot be elicited from non-existent sources or out of thin air.

It cannot be inferred from comparison of previous events, or from the thoughts and contemplations of the absolutes of competition, the slow market pace and fast market place and the changing ebbs and flows of markets, but must be obtained from people who have knowledge of the competitor's situation.

Therefore there are five kinds of intelligence gathering methods used;

1 localized people

2 internal people

3 people working for the opposition

4 people working for the market

5 people working for you; extinguished sources; and current sources.

When all five methods are used, and communication methods are kept secret, and there is alignment with thinking, then decisions and people's loyalty to the Cause with no fear of what lays ahead is apparent. Then it is called an ideal operation, and is the business's most prized possession.

- For local people, use the competitor's sale team.
- For internal people, use the competitor's sales leaders.
- For people working for the opposition, the market and for you, use the competitor's own intelligence gathering people.
- For extinguished sources use friendly supporters to spread mis-information to the competitors. For current sources use friendly supporters to return with reports.

Therefore, of those close to the sales team, none is closer than those who are engaged in intelligence gathering, no reward more generously given, and no matter in greater secrecy.

Only the wisest leader can use intelligence gathering processes and people.

Only the most benevolent and upright leader can use intelligence gathering processes and people, and only the most alert and observant person can get to the truth using use intelligence gathering processes and people.

It is subtle, subtle!

There is nowhere that intelligence gathering processes and people cannot be used.

If the use of intelligence gathering processes and knowledge of the people utilized is leaked before such activities begin, the intelligence gathering processes should cease and people be reassigned.

Generally, if a leader wants to engage in competitive market place activities, attack a strong competitor, nullify market participants, then the leader must have a complete knowledge of the competitor's leaders, sales team, and related personnel involved in market place participation.

You must have intelligence gathering processes and people go and seek them out and learn of the competitor.

You must seek competitor intelligence gathering processes and people. Persuade the people, and instruct and retain them.

Therefore people working for the opposition, the market and for you, can be obtained and used.

From their knowledge, you can obtain local and internal people.

From their knowledge, you can obtain extinguished sources and use friendly supporters to spread misinformation to the competitors.

From their knowledge, your current sources can be used as planned.

The leader must know these five practices of using competitor intelligence gathering processes and people to obtain information about the plans and activities of competing companies. This knowledge depends on the people working for the opposition, the market and for you.

Therefore, you must treat them with the utmost generosity.

In historic times, the rise of businesses was due to the utilisation of intelligence gathering processes and people capable of working in and with many and multiple businesses.

Therefore, knowledgeable businesses and good leaders who are able to obtain intelligent friendly supporters as intelligence gathering tools are certain for great achievements.

This is essential for competitive market place engagements, and what the sales team depends upon to move into markets.

Once you have read **The Martial Art of Sales** you're ready for the accompanying workbook

Workshop the Warlord: A Practical Training Guide for Sales Professionals

Workshop the Warlord: A Practical Training Guide for Sales Professionals has been written specifically to translate The Martial Art of Sales into direct actionable tasks for you and your sales team to mobilise the ancient wisdom of Sun Tzu throughout your business.

Anyone who has purchased *The Martial Art of Sales* for sales and marketing professionals, corporate leaders or executives, can use *Workshop the Warlord: A Practical Training Guide for Sales Professionals* series of templates and apply them to your business.

" *If you think the Martial Art of Sales was good; hang onto your hats! The accompanying workbook The Martial Art of Sales: Workshop the Warlord, takes Sun Tzu's calculating wisdom and turns it into specific actionable tasks that every sales person on the planet can do. It's straight forward and to the point. The book gets your head in the right place; the workbook delivers results.* "

The Original Translation of Sun Tzu's Art of War

1   Laying plans

2   Waging war

3   Attack by strategem

4   Tactical dispositions

5   Energy

6   Weak points and strong

7   Maneuvering

8   Variation in tactics

9   The Army on the march 10 Terrain

11   The nine situations

12   The attack by fire

13   The use of spies

1 Laying plans

1 Sun Tzu said: The art of war is of vital importance to the State.

2 It is a matter of life and death, a road either to safety or to ruin. Hence it is a subject of inquiry which can on no account be neglected.

3 The art of war, then, is governed by five constant factors, to be taken into account in one's deliberations, when seeking to determine the conditions obtaining in the field.

4 These are: (1) The Moral Law; (2) Heaven; (3) Earth; (4) The Commander; (5) Method and discipline.

5,6 The MORAL LAW causes the people to be in complete accord with their ruler, so that they will follow him regardless of their lives, undismayed by any danger.

7 HEAVEN signifies night and day, cold and heat, times and seasons.

8 EARTH comprises distances, great and small; danger and security; open ground and narrow passes; the chances of life and death.

9 The COMMANDER stands for the virtues of wisdom, sincerely, benevolence, courage and strictness.

10 By METHOD AND DISCIPLINE are to be understood the marshalling of the army in its proper subdivisions, the graduations of rank among the officers, the maintenance of roads by which supplies may reach the army, and the control of military expenditure.

11 These five heads should be familiar to every general: he who knows them will be victorious; he who knows them not will fail.

12 Therefore, in your deliberations, when seeking to determine the military conditions, let them be made the basis of a comparison, in this wise: --

13 (1) Which of the two sovereigns is imbued with the Moral law?

(2) Which of the two generals has most ability?

(3) With whom lie the advantages derived from Heaven and Earth?

(4) On which side is discipline most rigorously enforced?

(5) Which army is stronger?

(6) On which side are officers and men more highly trained?

(7) In which army is there the greater constancy both in reward and punishment?

14 By means of these seven considerations I can forecast victory or defeat.

15 The general that hearkens to my counsel and acts upon it, will conquer: --let such a one be retained in command! The general that hearkens not to my counsel nor acts upon it, will suffer defeat: --let such a one be dismissed!

16 While heading the profit of my counsel, avail yourself also of any helpful circumstances over and beyond the ordinary rules.

17 All warfare is based on deception.

18 Hence, when able to attack, we must seem unable; when using our forces, we must seem inactive; when we are near, we must make the enemy believe we are far away; when far away, we must make him believe we are near.

19 Hold out baits to entice the enemy. Feign disorder, and crush him.

20 If he is secure at all points, be prepared for him. If he is in superior strength, evade him.

21 If your opponent is of choleric temper, seek to irritate him. Pretend to be weak, that he may grow arrogant.

22 If he is taking his ease, give him no rest. If his forces are united, separate them.

23 Attack him where he is unprepared, appear where you are not expected.

24 These military devices, leading to victory, must not be divulged beforehand.

25 Now the general who wins a battle makes many calculations in his temple ere the battle is fought.

2 Waging war

1 Sun Tzu said: In the operations of war, where there are in the field a thousand swift chariots, as many heavy chariots, and a hundred thousand mail-clad soldiers, with provisions enough to carry them a thousand LI, the expenditure at home and at the front, including entertainment of guests, small items such as glue and paint, and sums spent on chariots and armor, will reach the total of a thousand ounces of silver per day. Such is the cost of raising an army of 100,000 men.

2 When you engage in actual fighting, if victory is long in coming, then men's weapons will grow dull and their ardor will be damped. If you lay siege to a town, you will exhaust your strength.

3 Again, if the campaign is protracted, the resources of the State will not be equal to the strain.

4 Now, when your weapons are dulled, your ardor damped, your strength exhausted and your treasure spent, other chieftains will spring up to take advantage of your extremity. Then no man, however wise, will be able to avert the consequences that must ensue.

5 Thus, though we have heard of stupid haste in war, cleverness has never been seen associated with long delays.

6 There is no instance of a country having benefited from prolonged warfare.

7 It is only one who is thoroughly acquainted with the evils of war that can thoroughly understand the profitable way of carrying it on.

8 The skillful soldier does not raise a second levy, neither are his supply- wagons loaded more than twice.

9 Bring war material with you from home, but forage on the enemy. Thus the army will have food enough for its needs.

10   Poverty of the State exchequer causes an army to be maintained by contributions from a distance. Contributing to maintain an army at a distance causes the people to be impoverished.

11   On the other hand, the proximity of an army causes prices to go up; and high prices cause the people's substance to be drained away.

12   When their substance is drained away, the peasantry will be afflicted by heavy exactions.

13,14 With this loss of substance and exhaustion of strength, the homes of the people will be stripped bare, and three-tenths of their income will be dissipated; while government expenses for broken chariots, worn-out horses, breast-plates and helmets, bows and arrows, spears and shields, protective mantles, draught-oxen and heavy wagons, will amount to four- tenths of its total revenue.

15   Hence a wise general makes a point of foraging on the enemy. One cart load of the enemy's provisions is equivalent to twenty of one's own, and likewise a single PICUL of his provender is equivalent to twenty from one's own store.

16   Now in order to kill the enemy, our men must be roused to anger; that there may be advantage from defeating the enemy, they must have their rewards.

17   Therefore in chariot fighting, when ten or more chariots have been taken, those should be rewarded who took the first. Our own flags should be substituted for those of the enemy, and the chariots mingled and used in conjunction with ours. The captured soldiers should be kindly treated and kept.

18   This is called, using the conquered foe to augment one's own strength.

19   In war, then, let your great object be victory, not lengthy campaigns.

20   Thus it may be known that the leader of armies is the arbiter of the people's fate, the man on whom it depends whether the nation shall be in peace or in peril

3 Attack by stratagem

1 Sun Tzu said: In the practical art of war, the best thing of all is to take the enemy's country whole and intact; to shatter and destroy it is not so good. So, too, it is better to recapture an army entire than to destroy it, to capture a regiment, a detachment or a company entire than to destroy them.

2 Hence to fight and conquer in all your battles is not supreme excellence; supreme excellence consists in breaking the enemy's resistance without fighting.

3 Thus the highest form of generalship is to balk the enemy's plans; the next best is to prevent the junction of the enemy's forces; the next in order is to attack the enemy's army in the field; and the worst policy of all is to besiege walled cities.

4 The rule is, not to besiege walled cities if it can possibly be avoided. The preparation of mantlets, movable shelters, and various implements of war, will take up three whole months; and the piling up of mounds over against the walls will take three months more.

5 The general, unable to control his irritation, will launch his men to the assault like swarming ants, with the result that one-third of his men are slain, while the town still remains untaken. Such are the disastrous effects of a siege.

6 Therefore the skilful leader subdues the enemy's troops without any fighting; he captures their cities without laying siege to them; he overthrows their kingdom without lengthy operations in the field.

7 With his forces intact he will dispute the mastery of the Empire, and thus, without losing a man, his triumph will be complete. This is the method of attacking by stratagem.

8 It is the rule in war, if our forces are ten to the enemy's one, to surround him; if five to one, to attack him; if twice as numerous, to divide our army into two.

9   If equally matched, we can offer battle; if slightly inferior in numbers, we can avoid the enemy; if quite unequal in every way, we can flee from him.

10 Hence, though an obstinate fight may be made by a small force, in the end it must be captured by the larger force.

11 Now the general is the bulwark of the State; if the bulwark is complete at all points; the State will be strong; if the bulwark is defective, the State will be weak.

12 There are three ways in which a ruler can bring misfortune upon his army:--

13 (1) By commanding the army to advance or to retreat, being ignorant of the fact that it cannot obey. This is called hobbling the army.

14 (2) By attempting to govern an army in the same way as he administers a kingdom, being ignorant of the conditions which obtain in an army. This causes restlessness in the soldier's minds.

15 (3) By employing the officers of his army without discrimination, through ignorance of the military principle of adaptation to circumstances. This shakes the confidence of the soldiers.

16 But when the army is restless and distrustful, trouble is sure to come from the other feudal princes. This is simply bringing anarchy into the army, and flinging victory away.

17 Thus we may know that there are five essentials for victory:

   (1)   He will win who knows when to fight and when not to fight.

   (2)   He will win who knows how to handle both superior and inferior forces.

   (3)   He will win whose army is animated by the same spirit throughout all its ranks.

   (4)   He will win who, prepared himself, waits to take the enemy unprepared.

(5) He will win who has military capacity and is not interfered with by the sovereign.

18 Hence the saying: If you know the enemy and know yourself, you need not fear the result of a hundred battles. If you know yourself but not the enemy, for every victory gained you will also suffer a defeat.

4 Tactical Dispositions

1   Sun Tzu said: The good fighters of old first put themselves beyond the possibility of defeat, and then waited for an opportunity of defeating the enemy.

2   To secure ourselves against defeat lies in our own hands, but the opportunity of defeating the enemy is provided by the enemy himself.

3   Thus the good fighter is able to secure himself against defeat, but cannot make certain of defeating the enemy.

4   Hence the saying: One may KNOW how to conquer without being able to DO it.

5   Security against defeat implies defensive tactics; ability to defeat the enemy means taking the offensive.

6   Standing on the defensive indicates insufficient strength; attacking, a superabundance of strength.

7   The general who is skilled in defense hides in the most secret recesses of the earth; he who is skilled in attack flashes forth from the topmost heights of heaven. Thus on the one hand we have ability to protect ourselves; on the other, a victory that is complete.

8   To see victory only when it is within the ken of the common herd is not the acme of excellence.

9   Neither is it the acme of excellence if you fight and conquer and the whole Empire says, "Well done!"

10   To lift an autumn hair is no sign of great strength; to see the sun and moon is no sign of sharp sight; to hear the noise of thunder is no sign of a quick ear.

11   What the ancients called a clever fighter is one who not only wins, but excels in winning with ease.

12 Hence his victories bring him neither reputation for wisdom nor credit for courage.

13 He wins his battles by making no mistakes. Making no mistakes is what establishes the certainty of victory, for it means conquering an enemy that is already defeated.

14 Hence the skilful fighter puts himself into a position which makes defeat impossible, and does not miss the moment for defeating the enemy.

15 Thus it is that in war the victorious strategist only seeks battle after the victory has been won, whereas he who is destined to defeat first fights and afterwards looks for victory.

16 The consummate leader cultivates the moral law, and strictly adheres to method and discipline; thus it is in his power to control success.

17 In respect of military method, we have, firstly, Measurement; secondly, Estimation of quantity; thirdly, Calculation; fourthly, Balancing of chances; fifthly, Victory.

18 Measurement owes its existence to Earth; Estimation of quantity to Measurement; Calculation to Estimation of quantity; Balancing of chances to Calculation; and Victory to Balancing of chances.

19 A victorious army opposed to a routed one, is as a pound's weight placed in the scale against a single grain.

20 The onrush of a conquering force is like the bursting of pent-up waters into a chasm a thousand fathoms deep.

5 Energy

1 Sun Tzu said: The control of a large force is the same principle as the control of a few men: it is merely a question of dividing up their numbers.

2 Fighting with a large army under your command is nowise different from fighting with a small one: it is merely a question of instituting signs and signals.

3 To ensure that your whole host may withstand the brunt of the enemy's attack and remain unshaken - this is effected by maneuvers direct and indirect.

4 That the impact of your army may be like a grindstone dashed against an egg - this is effected by the science of weak points and strong.

5 In all fighting, the direct method may be used for joining battle, but indirect methods will be needed in order to secure victory.

6 Indirect tactics, efficiently applied, are inexhaustible as Heaven and Earth, unending as the flow of rivers and streams; like the sun and moon, they end but to begin anew; like the four seasons, they pass away to return once more.

7 There are not more than five musical notes, yet the combinations of these five give rise to more melodies than can ever be heard.

8 There are not more than five primary colors (blue, yellow, red, white, and black), yet in combination they produce more hues than can ever been seen.

9 There are not more than five cardinal tastes (sour, acrid, salt, sweet, bitter), yet combinations of them yield more flavors than can ever be tasted.

10 In battle, there are not more than two methods of attack - the direct and the indirect; yet these two in combination give rise to an endless series of maneuvers.

11 The direct and the indirect lead on to each other in turn. It is like moving in a circle - you never come to an end. Who can exhaust the possibilities of their combination?

12 The onset of troops is like the rush of a torrent which will even roll stones along in its course.

13 The quality of decision is like the well-timed swoop of a falcon which enables it to strike and destroy its victim.

14 Therefore the good fighter will be terrible in his onset, and prompt in his decision.

15 Energy may be likened to the bending of a crossbow; decision, to the releasing of a trigger.

16 Amid the turmoil and tumult of battle, there may be seeming disorder and yet no real disorder at all; amid confusion and chaos, your array may be without head or tail, yet it will be proof against defeat.

17 Simulated disorder postulates perfect discipline, simulated fear postulates courage; simulated weakness postulates strength.

18 Hiding order beneath the cloak of disorder is simply a question of subdivision; concealing courage under a show of timidity presupposes a fund of latent energy; masking strength with weakness is to be effected by tactical dispositions.

19 Thus one who is skilful at keeping the enemy on the move maintains deceitful appearances, according to which the enemy will act. He sacrifices something, that the enemy may snatch at it.

20 By holding out baits, he keeps him on the march; then with a body of picked men he lies in wait for him.

21 The clever combatant looks to the effect of combined energy, and does not require too much from individuals. Hence his ability to pick out the right men and utilize combined energy.

22 When he utilizes combined energy, his fighting men become as it were like unto rolling logs or stones. For it is the nature of a log or stone to remain motionless on level ground, and to move when on a slope; if four-cornered, to come to a standstill, but if round-shaped, to go rolling down.

23 Thus the energy developed by good fighting men is as the momentum of a round stone rolled down a mountain thousands of feet in height. So much on the subject of energy.

6 Weak points and strong

1 Sun Tzu said: Whoever is first in the field and awaits the coming of the enemy, will be fresh for the fight; whoever is second in the field and has to hasten to battle will arrive exhausted.

2 Therefore the clever combatant imposes his will on the enemy, but does not allow the enemy's will to be imposed on him.

3 By holding out advantages to him, he can cause the enemy to approach of his own accord; or, by inflicting damage, he can make it impossible for the enemy to draw near.

4 If the enemy is taking his ease, he can harass him; if well supplied with food, he can starve him out; if quietly encamped, he can force him to move.

5 Appear at points which the enemy must hasten to defend; march swiftly to places where you are not expected.

6 An army may march great distances without distress, if it marches through country where the enemy is not.

7 You can be sure of succeeding in your attacks if you only attack places which are undefended. You can ensure the safety of your defense if you only hold positions that cannot be attacked.

8 Hence that general is skilful in attack whose opponent does not know what to defend; and he is skilful in defense whose opponent does not know what to attack.

9 O divine art of subtlety and secrecy! Through you we learn to be invisible, through you inaudible; and hence we can hold the enemy's fate in our hands.

10 You may advance and be absolutely irresistible, if you make for the enemy's weak points; you may retire and be safe from pursuit if your movements are more rapid than those of the enemy.

11 If we wish to fight, the enemy can be forced to an engagement even though he be sheltered behind a high rampart and a deep

ditch. All we need do is attack some other place that he will be obliged to relieve.

12 If we do not wish to fight, we can prevent the enemy from engaging us even though the lines of our encampment be merely traced out on the ground. All we need do is to throw something odd and unaccountable in his way.

13 By discovering the enemy's dispositions and remaining invisible ourselves, we can keep our forces concentrated, while the enemy's must be divided.

14 We can form a single united body, while the enemy must split up into fractions. Hence there will be a whole pitted against separate parts of a whole, which means that we shall be many to the enemy's few.

15 And if we are able thus to attack an inferior force with a superior one, our opponents will be in dire straits.

16 The spot where we intend to fight must not be made known; for then the enemy will have to prepare against a possible attack at several different points; and his forces being thus distributed in many directions, the numbers we shall have to face at any given point will be proportionately few.

17 For should the enemy strengthen his van, he will weaken his rear; should he strengthen his rear, he will weaken his van; should he strengthen his left, he will weaken his right; should he strengthen his right, he will weaken his left. If he sends reinforcements everywhere, he will everywhere be weak.

18 Numerical weakness comes from having to prepare against possible attacks; numerical strength, from compelling our adversary to make these preparations against us.

19 Knowing the place and the time of the coming battle, we may concentrate from the greatest distances in order to fight.

20 But if neither time nor place be known, then the left wing will be impotent to succor the right, the right equally impotent to succor the left, the van unable to relieve the rear, or the rear to support the van. How much more so if the furthest portions of the army are anything under a hundred LI apart, and even the nearest are separated by several LI!

21 Though according to my estimate the soldiers of Yueh exceed our own in number, that shall advantage them nothing in the matter of victory. I say then that victory can be achieved.

22 Though the enemy be stronger in numbers, we may prevent him from fighting. Scheme so as to discover his plans and the likelihood of their success.

23 Rouse him, and learn the principle of his activity or inactivity. Force him to reveal himself, so as to find out his vulnerable spots.

24 Carefully compare the opposing army with your own, so that you may know where strength is superabundant and where it is deficient.

25 In making tactical dispositions, the highest pitch you can attain is to conceal them; conceal your dispositions, and you will be safe from the prying of the subtlest spies, from the machinations of the wisest brains.

26 How victory may be produced for them out of the enemy's own tactics--that is what the multitude cannot comprehend.

27 All men can see the tactics whereby I conquer, but what none can see is the strategy out of which victory is evolved.

28 Do not repeat the tactics which have gained you one victory, but let your methods be regulated by the infinite variety of circumstances.

29 Military tactics are like unto water; for water in its natural course runs away from high places and hastens downwards.

30   So in war, the way is to avoid what is strong and to strike at what is weak.

31   Water shapes its course according to the nature of the ground over which it flows; the soldier works out his victory in relation to the foe whom he is facing.

32   Therefore, just as water retains no constant shape, so in warfare there are no constant conditions.

33   He who can modify his tactics in relation to his opponent and thereby succeed in winning, may be called a heaven- born captain.

34   The five elements (water, fire, wood, metal, earth) are not always equally predominant;

7 Maneuvering

1 Sun Tzu said: In war, the general receives his commands from the sovereign.

2 Having collected an army and concentrated his forces, he must blend and harmonize the different elements thereof before pitching his camp.

3 After that, comes tactical maneuvering, than which there is nothing more difficult. The difficulty of tactical maneuvering consists in turning the devious into the direct, and misfortune into gain.

4 Thus, to take a long and circuitous route, after enticing the enemy out of the way, and though starting after him, to contrive to reach the goal before him, shows knowledge of the artifice of DEVIATION.

5 Maneuvering with an army is advantageous; with an undisciplined multitude, most dangerous.

6 If you set a fully equipped army in march in order to snatch an advantage, the chances are that you will be too late. On the other hand, to detach a flying column for the purpose involves the sacrifice of its baggage and stores.

7 Thus, if you order your men to roll up their buff-coats, and make forced marches without halting day or night, covering double the usual distance at a stretch, doing a hundred LI in order to wrest an advantage, the leaders of all your three divisions will fall into the hands of the enemy.

8 The stronger men will be in front, the jaded ones will fall behind, and on this plan only one-tenth of your army will reach its destination.

9 If you march fifty LI in order to outmaneuver the enemy, you will lose the leader of your first division, and only half your force will reach the goal.

10 If you march thirty LI with the same object, two-thirds of your army will arrive.

11 We may take it then that an army without its baggage- train is lost; without provisions it is lost; without bases of supply it is lost.

12 We cannot enter into alliances until we are acquainted with the designs of our neighbors.

13 We are not fit to lead an army on the march unless we are familiar with the face of the country--its mountains and forests, its pitfalls and precipices, its marshes and swamps.

14 We shall be unable to turn natural advantage to account unless we make use of local guides.

15 In war, practice dissimulation, and you will succeed.

16 Whether to concentrate or to divide your troops, must be decided by circumstances.

17 Let your rapidity be that of the wind, your compactness that of the forest.

18 In raiding and plundering be like fire, is immovability like a mountain.

19 Let your plans be dark and impenetrable as night, and when you move, fall like a thunderbolt.

20 When you plunder a countryside, let the spoil be divided amongst your men; when you capture new territory, cut it up into allotments for the benefit of the soldiery.

21 Ponder and deliberate before you make a move.

22 He will conquer who has learnt the artifice of deviation. Such is the art of maneuvering.

23 The Book of Army Management says: On the field of battle, the spoken word does not carry far enough: hence the institution

of gongs and drums. Nor can ordinary objects be seen clearly enough: hence the institution of banners and flags.

24 Gongs and drums, banners and flags, are means whereby the ears and eyes of the host may be focused on one particular point.

25 The host thus forming a single united body, is it impossible either for the brave to advance alone, or for the cowardly to retreat alone. This is the art of handling large masses of men.

26 In night-fighting, then, make much use of signal-fires and drums, and in fighting by day, of flags and banners, as a means of influencing the ears and eyes of your army.

27 A whole army may be robbed of its spirit; a commander-in-chief may be robbed of his presence of mind.

28 Now a soldier's spirit is keenest in the morning; by noonday it has begun to flag; and in the evening, his mind is bent only on returning to camp.

29 A clever general, therefore, avoids an army when its spirit is keen, but attacks it when it is sluggish and inclined to return. This is the art of studying moods.

30 Disciplined and calm, to await the appearance of disorder and hubbub amongst the enemy:--this is the art of retaining self-possession.

31 To be near the goal while the enemy is still far from it, to wait at ease while the enemy is toiling and struggling, to be well-fed while the enemy is famished:--this is the art of husbanding one's strength.

32 To refrain from intercepting an enemy whose banners are in perfect order, to refrain from attacking an army drawn up in calm and confident array:-- this is the art of studying circumstances.

33 It is a military axiom not to advance uphill against the enemy, nor to oppose him when he comes downhill.

34 Do not pursue an enemy who simulates flight; do not attack soldiers whose temper is keen.

35 Do not swallow bait offered by the enemy. Do not interfere with an army that is returning home.

36 When you surround an army, leave an outlet free. Do not press a desperate foe too hard.

37 Such is the art of warfare.

8 Variation in tactics

1 Sun Tzu said: In war, the general receives his commands from the sovereign, collects his army and concentrates his forces.

2 When in difficult country, do not encamp. In country where high roads intersect, join hands with your allies. Do not linger in dangerously isolated positions. In hemmed-in situations, you must resort to stratagem. In desperate position, you must fight.

3 There are roads which must not be followed, armies which must be not attacked, towns which must not be besieged, positions which must not be contested, commands of the sovereign which must not be obeyed.

4 The general who thoroughly understands the advantages that accompany variation of tactics knows how to handle his troops.

5 The general who does not understand these, may be well acquainted with the configuration of the country, yet he will not be able to turn his knowledge to practical account.

6 So, the student of war who is unversed in the art of war of varying his plans, even though he be acquainted with the Five Advantages, will fail to make the best use of his men.

7 Hence in the wise leader's plans, considerations of advantage and of disadvantage will be blended together.

8 If our expectation of advantage be tempered in this way, we may succeed in accomplishing the essential part of our schemes.

9 If, on the other hand, in the midst of difficulties we are always ready to seize an advantage, we may extricate ourselves from misfortune.

10 Reduce the hostile chiefs by inflicting damage on them; and make trouble for them, and keep them constantly engaged; hold out specious allurements, and make them rush to any given point.

11 The art of war teaches us to rely not on the likelihood of the enemy's not coming, but on our own readiness to receive him; not on the chance of his not attacking, but rather on the fact that we have made our position unassailable.

12 There are five dangerous faults which may affect a general:

(1) Recklessness, which leads to destruction;

(2) cowardice, which leads to capture;

(3) a hasty temper, which can be provoked by insults;

(4) a delicacy of honor which is sensitive to shame;

(5) over-solicitude for his men, which exposes him to worry and trouble.

13 These are the five besetting sins of a general, ruinous to the conduct of war.

14 When an army is overthrown and its leader slain, the cause will surely be found among these five dangerous faults. Let them be a subject of meditation.

9 The army on the march

1   Sun Tzu said: We come now to the question of encamping the army, and observing signs of the enemy. Pass quickly over mountains, and keep in the neighborhood of valleys.

2   Camp in high places, facing the sun. Do not climb heights in order to fight. So much for mountain warfare.

3   After crossing a river, you should get far away from it.

4   When an invading force crosses a river in its onward march, do not advance to meet it in mid-stream. It will be best to let half the army get across, and then deliver your attack.

5   If you are anxious to fight, you should not go to meet the invader near a river which he has to cross.

6   Moor your craft higher up than the enemy, and facing the sun. Do not move up-stream to meet the enemy. So much for river warfare.

7   In crossing salt-marshes, your sole concern should be to get over them quickly, without

8   If forced to fight in a salt-marsh, you should have water and grass near you, and get your back to a clump of trees. So much for operations in salt- marches.

9   In dry, level country, take up an easily accessible position with rising ground to your right and on your rear, so that the danger may be in front, and safety lie behind. So much for campaigning in flat country.

10   These are the four useful branches of military knowledge which enabled the Yellow Emperor to vanquish four several sovereigns.

11   All armies prefer high ground to low and sunny places to dark.

12   If you are careful of your men, and camp on hard ground, the army will be free from disease of every kind, and this will spell victory.

13 When you come to a hill or a bank, occupy the sunny side, with the slope on your right rear. Thus you will at once act for the benefit of your soldiers and utilize the natural advantages of the ground.

14 When, in consequence of heavy rains up-country, a river which you wish to ford is swollen and flecked with foam, you must wait until it subsides.

15 Country in which there are precipitous cliffs with torrents running between, deep natural hollows, confined places, tangled thickets, quagmires and crevasses, should be left with all possible speed and not approached.

16 While we keep away from such places, we should get the enemy to approach them; while we face them, we should let the enemy have them on his rear.

17 If in the neighborhood of your camp there should be any hilly country, ponds surrounded by aquatic grass, hollow basins filled with reeds, or woods with thick undergrowth, they must be carefully routed out and searched; for these are places where men in ambush or insidious spies are likely to be lurking.

18 When the enemy is close at hand and remains quiet, he is relying on the natural strength of his position.

19 When he keeps aloof and tries to provoke a battle, he is anxious for the other side to advance.

20 If his place of encampment is easy of access, he is tendering a bait.

21 Movement amongst the trees of a forest shows that the enemy is advancing. The appearance of a number of screens in the midst of thick grass means that the enemy wants to make us suspicious.

22 The rising of birds in their flight is the sign of an ambuscade. Startled beasts indicate that a sudden attack is coming.

23 When there is dust rising in a high column, it is the sign of chariots advancing; when the dust is low, but spread over a wide area, it betokens the approach of infantry. When it branches out in different directions, it shows that parties have been sent to collect firewood. A few clouds of dust moving to and fro signify that the army is encamping.

24 Humble words and increased preparations are signs that the enemy is about to advance. Violent language and driving forward as if to the attack are signs that he will retreat.

25 When the light chariots come out first and take up a position on the wings, it is a sign that the enemy is forming for battle.

26 Peace proposals unaccompanied by a sworn covenant indicate a plot.

27 When there is much running about and the soldiers fall into rank, it means that the critical moment has come.

28 When some are seen advancing and some retreating, it is a lure.

29 When the soldiers stand leaning on their spears, they are faint from want of food.

30 If those who are sent to draw water begin by drinking themselves, the army is suffering from thirst.

31 If the enemy sees an advantage to be gained and makes no effort to secure it, the soldiers are exhausted.

32 If birds gather on any spot, it is unoccupied. Clamor by night betokens nervousness.

33 If there is disturbance in the camp, the general's authority is weak. If the banners and flags are shifted about, sedition is afoot. If the officers are angry, it means that the men are weary.

34 When an army feeds its horses with grain and kills its cattle for food, and when the men do not hang their cooking-pots over the camp- fires, showing that they will not return to their tents, you may know that they are determined to fight to the death.

35 The sight of men whispering together in small knots or speaking in subdued tones points to disaffection amongst the rank and file.

36 Too frequent rewards signify that the enemy is at the end of his resources; too many punishments betray a condition of dire distress.

37 To begin by bluster, but afterwards to take fright at the enemy's numbers, shows a supreme lack of intelligence.

38 When envoys are sent with compliments in their mouths, it is a sign that the enemy wishes for a truce.

39 If the enemy's troops march up angrily and remain facing ours for a long time without either joining battle or taking themselves off again, the situation is one that demands great vigilance and circumspection.

40 If our troops are no more in number than the enemy, that is amply sufficient; it only means that no direct attack can be made. What we can do is simply to concentrate all our available strength, keep a close watch on the enemy, and obtain reinforcements.

41 He who exercises no forethought but makes light of his opponents is sure to be captured by them.

42 If soldiers are punished before they have grown attached to you, they will not prove submissive; and, unless submissive, then will be practically useless. If, when the soldiers have become attached to you, punishments are not enforced, they will still be unless.

43 Therefore soldiers must be treated in the first instance with humanity, but kept under control by means of iron discipline. This is a certain road to victory.

44 If in training soldiers commands are habitually enforced, the army will be well-disciplined; if not, its discipline will be bad. 45. If a general shows confidence in his men but always insists on his orders being obeyed, the gain will be mutual.

10 Terrain

1 Sun Tzu said: We may distinguish six kinds of terrain, to wit: (1) Accessible ground; (2) entangling ground; (3) temporizing ground; (4) narrow passes; (5) precipitous heights; (6) positions at a great distance from the enemy.

2 Ground which can be freely traversed by both sides is called ACCESSIBLE.

3 With regard to ground of this nature, be before the enemy in occupying the raised and sunny spots, and carefully guard your line of supplies. Then you will be able to fight with advantage.

4 Ground which can be abandoned but is hard to re-occupy is called ENTANGLING.

5 From a position of this sort, if the enemy is unprepared, you may sally forth and defeat him. But if the enemy is prepared for your coming, and you fail to defeat him, then, return being impossible, disaster will ensue.

6 When the position is such that neither side will gain by making the first move, it is called TEMPORIZING ground.

7 In a position of this sort, even though the enemy should offer us an attractive bait, it will be advisable not to stir forth, but rather to retreat, thus enticing the enemy in his turn; then, when part of his army has come out, we may deliver our attack with advantage.

8 With regard to NARROW PASSES, if you can occupy them first, let them be strongly garrisoned and await the advent of the enemy.

9 Should the army forestall you in occupying a pass, do not go after him if the pass is fully garrisoned, but only if it is weakly garrisoned.

10 With regard to PRECIPITOUS HEIGHTS, if you are beforehand with your adversary, you should occupy the raised and sunny spots, and there wait for him to come up.

11   If the enemy has occupied them before you, do not follow him, but retreat and try to entice him away.

12   If you are situated at a great distance from the enemy, and the strength of the two armies is equal, it is not easy to provoke a battle, and fighting will be to your disadvantage.

13   These six are the principles connected with Earth. The general who has attained a responsible post must be careful to study them.

14   Now an army is exposed to six several calamities, not arising from natural causes, but from faults for which the general is responsible. These are: (1) Flight; (2) insubordination; (3) collapse; (4) ruin; (5) disorganization; (6) rout.

15   Other conditions being equal, if one force is hurled against another ten times its size, the result will be the FLIGHT of the former.

16   When the common soldiers are too strong and their officers too weak, the result is INSUBORDINATION. When the officers are too strong and the common soldiers too weak, the result is COLLAPSE.

17   When the higher officers are angry and insubordinate, and on meeting the enemy give battle on their own account from a feeling of resentment, before the commander-in-chief can tell whether or no he is in a position to fight, the result is RUIN.

18   When the general is weak and without authority; when his orders are not clear and distinct; when there are no fixes duties assigned to officers and men, and the ranks are formed in a slovenly haphazard manner, the result is utter DISORGANIZATION.

19   When a general, unable to estimate the enemy's strength, allows an inferior force to engage a larger one, or hurls a weak detachment against a powerful one, and neglects to place picked soldiers in the front rank, the result must be ROUT.

20 These are six ways of courting defeat, which must be carefully noted by the general who has attained a responsible post.

21 The natural formation of the country is the soldier's best ally; but a power of estimating the adversary, of controlling the forces of victory, and of shrewdly calculating difficulties, dangers and distances, constitutes the test of a great general.

22 He who knows these things, and in fighting puts his knowledge into practice, will win his battles. He who knows them not, nor practices them, will surely be defeated.

23 If fighting is sure to result in victory, then you must fight, even though the ruler forbid it; if fighting will not result in victory, then you must not fight even at the ruler's bidding.

24 The general who advances without coveting fame and retreats without fearing disgrace, whose only thought is to protect his country and do good service for his sovereign, is the jewel of the kingdom.

25 Regard your soldiers as your children, and they will follow you into the deepest valleys; look upon them as your own beloved sons, and they will stand by you even unto death.

26 If, however, you are indulgent, but unable to make your authority felt; kind- hearted, but unable to enforce your commands; and incapable, moreover, of quelling disorder: then your soldiers must be likened to spoilt children; they are useless for any practical purpose.

27 If we know that our own men are in a condition to attack, but are unaware that the enemy is not open to attack, we have gone only halfway towards victory.

28 If we know that the enemy is open to attack, but are unaware that our own men are not in a condition to attack, we have gone only halfway towards victory.

29 If we know that the enemy is open to attack, and also know that our men are in a condition to attack, but are unaware that the nature of the ground makes fighting impracticable, we have still gone only halfway towards victory.

30 Hence the experienced soldier, once in motion, is never bewildered; once he has broken camp, he is never at a loss.

31 Hence the saying: If you know the enemy and know yourself, your victory will not stand in doubt; if you know Heaven and know Earth, you may make your victory complete.

11 The nine situations

1   Sun Tzu said: The art of war recognizes nine varieties of ground: (1) Dispersive ground; (2) facile ground; (3) contentious ground; (4) open ground; (5) ground of intersecting highways; (6) serious ground; (7) difficult ground; (8) hemmed-in ground; (9) desperate ground.

2   When a chieftain is fighting in his own territory, it is dispersive ground.

3   When he has penetrated into hostile territory, but to no great distance, it is facile ground.

4   Ground the possession of which imports great advantage to either side, is contentious ground.

5   Ground on which each side has liberty of movement is open ground.

6   Ground which forms the key to three contiguous states, so that he who occupies it first has most of the Empire at his command, is a ground of intersecting highways.

7   When an army has penetrated into the heart of a hostile country, leaving a number of fortified cities in its rear, it is serious ground.

8   Mountain forests, rugged steeps, marshes and fens--all country that is hard to traverse: this is difficult ground.

9   Ground which is reached through narrow gorges, and from which we can only retire by tortuous paths, so that a small number of the enemy would suffice to crush a large body of our men: this is hemmed in ground.

10   Ground on which we can only be saved from destruction by fighting without delay, is desperate ground.

11   On dispersive ground, therefore, fight not. On facile ground, halt not. On contentious ground, attack not.

12 On open ground, do not try to block the enemy's way. On the ground of intersecting highways, join hands with your allies.

13 On serious ground, gather in plunder. In difficult ground, keep steadily on the march.

14 On hemmed-in ground, resort to stratagem. On desperate ground, fight.

15 Those who were called skillful leaders of old knew how to drive a wedge between the enemy's front and rear; to prevent co-operation between his large and small divisions; to hinder the good troops from rescuing the bad, the officers from rallying their men.

16 When the enemy's men were united, they managed to keep them in disorder.

17 When it was to their advantage, they made a forward move; when otherwise, they stopped still.

18 If asked how to cope with a great host of the enemy in orderly array and on the point of marching to the attack, I should say: "Begin by seizing something which your opponent holds dear; then he will be amenable to your will."

19 Rapidity is the essence of war: take advantage of the enemy's unreadiness, make your way by unexpected routes, and attack unguarded spots.

20 The following are the principles to be observed by an invading force: The further you penetrate into a country, the greater will be the solidarity of your troops, and thus the defenders will not prevail against you.

21 Make forays in fertile country in order to supply your army with food.

22 Carefully study the well-being of your men, and do not overtax them. Concentrate your energy and hoard your strength. Keep your army continually on the move, and devise unfathomable plans.

23 Throw your soldiers into positions whence there is no escape, and they will prefer death to flight. If they will face death, there is nothing they may not achieve. Officers and men alike will put forth their uttermost strength.

24 Soldiers when in desperate straits lose the sense of fear. If there is no place of refuge, they will stand firm. If they are in hostile country, they will show a stubborn front. If there is no help for it, they will fight hard.

25 Thus, without waiting to be marshaled, the soldiers will be constantly on the qui vive; without waiting to be asked, they will do your will; without restrictions, they will be faithful; without giving orders, they can be trusted.

26 Prohibit the taking of omens, and do away with superstitious doubts. Then, until death itself comes, no calamity need be feared.

27 If our soldiers are not overburdened with money, it is not because they have a distaste for riches; if their lives are not unduly long, it is not because they are disinclined to longevity.

28 On the day they are ordered out to battle, your soldiers may weep, those sitting up bedewing their garments, and those lying down letting the tears run down their cheeks. But let them once be brought to bay, and they will display the courage of a Chu or a Kuei.

29 The skillful tactician may be likened to the SHUAI-JAN. Now the SHUAI- JAN is a snake that is found in the Ch`ang mountains. Strike at its head, and you will be attacked by its tail; strike at its tail, and you will be attacked by its head; strike at its middle, and you will be attacked by head and tail both.

30 Asked if an army can be made to imitate the SHUAI-JAN, I should answer, Yes. For the men of Wu and the men of Yueh are enemies; yet if they are crossing a river in the same boat and are caught by a storm, they will come to each other's assistance just as the left hand helps the right.

31 Hence it is not enough to put one's trust in the tethering of horses, and the burying of chariot wheels in the ground.

32 The principle on which to manage an army is to set up one standard of courage which all must reach.

33 How to make the best of both strong and weak--that is a question involving the proper use of ground.

34 Thus the skillful general conducts his army just as though he were leading a single man, willy-nilly, by the hand.

35 It is the business of a general to be quiet and thus ensure secrecy; upright and just, and thus maintain order.

36 He must be able to mystify his officers and men by false reports and appearances, and thus keep them in total ignorance.

37 By altering his arrangements and changing his plans, he keeps the enemy without definite knowledge. By shifting his camp and taking circuitous routes, he prevents the enemy from anticipating his purpose.

38 At the critical moment, the leader of an army acts like one who has climbed up a height and then kicks away the ladder behind him. He carries his men deep into hostile territory before he shows his hand.

39 He burns his boats and breaks his cooking-pots; like a shepherd driving a flock of sheep, he drives his men this way and that, and nothing knows whither he is going.

40 To muster his host and bring it into danger:--this may be termed the business of the general.

41 The different measures suited to the nine varieties of ground; the expediency of aggressive or defensive tactics; and the fundamental laws of human nature: these are things that must most certainly be studied.

42 When invading hostile territory, the general principle is, that penetrating deeply brings cohesion; penetrating but a short way means dispersion.

43 When you leave your own country behind, and take your army across neighborhood territory, you find yourself on critical ground. When there are means of communication on all four sides, the ground is one of intersecting highways.

44 When you penetrate deeply into a country, it is serious ground. When you penetrate but a little way, it is facile ground.

45 When you have the enemy's strongholds on your rear, and narrow passes in front, it is hemmed-in ground. When there is no place of refuge at all, it is desperate ground.

46 Therefore, on dispersive ground, I would inspire my men with unity of purpose. On facile ground, I would see that there is close connection between all parts of my army.

48 On open ground, I would keep a vigilant eye on my defenses. On ground of intersecting highways, I would consolidate my alliances.

49 On serious ground, I would try to ensure a continuous stream of supplies. On difficult ground, I would keep pushing on along the road.

50 On hemmed-in ground, I would block any way of retreat. On desperate ground, I would proclaim to my soldiers the hopelessness of saving their lives.

51 For it is the soldier's disposition to offer an obstinate resistance when surrounded, to fight hard when he cannot help himself, and to obey promptly when he has fallen into danger.

52 We cannot enter into alliance with neighboring princes until we are acquainted with their designs. We are not fit to lead an army on the march unless we are familiar with the face of the country--its mountains and forests, its pitfalls and precipices, its marshes and swamps. We shall be unable to turn natural advantages to account unless we make use of local guides.

53 To be ignored of any one of the following four or five principles does not befit a warlike prince.

54 When a warlike prince attacks a powerful state, his generalship shows itself in preventing the concentration of the enemy's forces. He overawes his opponents, and their allies are prevented from joining against him.

55 Hence he does not strive to ally himself with all and sundry, nor does he foster the power of other states. He carries out his own secret designs, keeping his antagonists in awe. Thus he is able to capture their cities and overthrow their kingdoms.

56 Bestow rewards without regard to rule, issue orders without regard to previous arrangements; and you will be able to handle a whole army as though you had to do with but a single man.

57 Confront your soldiers with the deed itself; never let them know your design. When the outlook is bright, bring it before their eyes; but tell them nothing when the situation is gloomy.

58 Place your army in deadly peril, and it will survive; plunge it into desperate straits, and it will come off in safety.

59 For it is precisely when a force has fallen into harm's way that is capable of striking a blow for victory.

60 Success in warfare is gained by carefully accommodating ourselves to the enemy's purpose.

61 By persistently hanging on the enemy's flank, we shall succeed in the long run in killing the commander-in-chief.

62 This is called ability to accomplish a thing by sheer cunning.

63 On the day that you take up your command, block the frontier passes, destroy the official tallies, and stop the passage of all emissaries.

64 Be stern in the council-chamber, so that you may control the situation.

65 If the enemy leaves a door open, you must rush in.

66 Forestall your opponent by seizing what he holds dear, and subtly contrive to time his arrival on the ground.

67 Walk in the path defined by rule, and accommodate yourself to the enemy until you can fight a decisive battle.

68 At first, then, exhibit the coyness of a maiden, until the enemy gives you an opening; afterwards emulate the rapidity of a running hare, and it will be too late for the enemy to oppose you.

12 The attack by fire

1   Sun Tzu said: There are five ways of attacking with fire. The first is to burn soldiers in their camp; the second is to burn stores; [the third is to burn baggage trains; the fourth is to burn arsenals and magazines; the fifth is to hurl dropping fire amongst the enemy.

2   In order to carry out an attack, we must have means available. the material for raising fire should always be kept in readiness.

3   There is a proper season for making attacks with fire, and special days for starting a conflagration.

4   The proper season is when the weather is very dry; the special days are those when the moon is in the constellations of the Sieve, the Wall, the Wing or the Cross-bar; for these four are all days of rising wind.

5   In attacking with fire, one should be prepared to meet five possible developments:

6   (1) When fire breaks out inside to enemy's camp, respond at once with an attack from without.

7   (2) If there is an outbreak of fire, but the enemy's soldiers remain quiet, bide your time and do not attack.

8   (3) When the force of the flames has reached its height, follow it up with an attack, if that is practicable; if not, stay where you are.

9   (4) If it is possible to make an assault with fire from without, do not wait for it to break out within, but deliver your attack at a favorable moment.

10   (5) When you start a fire, be to windward of it. Do not attack from the leeward.

11   A wind that rises in the daytime lasts long, but a night breeze soon falls.

12 In every army, the five developments connected with fire must be known, the movements of the stars calculated, and a watch kept for the proper days.

13 Hence those who use fire as an aid to the attack show intelligence; those who use water as an aid to the attack gain an accession of strength.

14 By means of water, an enemy may be intercepted, but not robbed of all his belongings.

15 Unhappy is the fate of one who tries to win his battles and succeed in his attacks without cultivating the spirit of enterprise; for the result is waste of time and general stagnation.

16 Hence the saying: The enlightened ruler lays his plans well ahead; the good general cultivates his resources.

17 Move not unless you see an advantage; use not your troops unless there is something to be gained; fight not unless the position is critical.

18 No ruler should put troops into the field merely to gratify his own spleen; no general should fight a battle simply out of pique.

19 If it is to your advantage, make a forward move; if not, stay where you are.

20 Anger may in time change to gladness; vexation may be succeeded by content.

21 But a kingdom that has once been destroyed can never come again into being; nor can the dead ever be brought back to life.

22 Hence the enlightened ruler is heedful, and the good general full of caution. This is the way to keep a country at peace and an army intact.

13 The use of spies

1 Sun Tzu said: Raising a host of a hundred thousand men and marching them great distances entails heavy loss on the people and a drain on the resources of the State. The daily expenditure will amount to a thousand ounces of silver. There will be commotion at home and abroad, and men will drop down exhausted on the highways. As many as seven hundred thousand families will be impeded in their labor.

2 Hostile armies may face each other for years, striving for the victory which is decided in a single day. This being so, to remain in ignorance of the enemy's condition simply because one grudges the outlay of a hundred ounces of silver in honors and emoluments, is the height of inhumanity.

3 One who acts thus is no leader of men, no present help to his sovereign, no master of victory.

4 Thus, what enables the wise sovereign and the good general to strike and conquer, and achieve things beyond the reach of ordinary men, is FOREKNOWLEDGE.

5 Now this foreknowledge cannot be elicited from spirits; it cannot be obtained inductively from experience, nor by any deductive calculation.

6 Knowledge of the enemy's dispositions can only be obtained from other men.

7 Hence the use of spies, of whom there are five classes: (1) Local spies; (2) inward spies; (3) converted spies; (4) doomed spies; (5) surviving spies.

8 When these five kinds of spy are all at work, none can discover the secret system. This is called "divine manipulation of the threads." It is the sovereign's most precious faculty.

9 Having LOCAL SPIES means employing the services of the inhabitants of a district.

10 Having INWARD SPIES, making use of officials of the enemy.

11 Having CONVERTED SPIES, getting hold of the enemy's spies and using them for our own purposes.

12 Having DOOMED SPIES, doing certain things openly for purposes of deception, and allowing our spies to know of them and report them to the enemy.

13 SURVIVING SPIES, finally, are those who bring back news from the enemy's camp.

14 Hence it is that which none in the whole army are more intimate relations to be maintained than with spies. None should be more liberally rewarded. In no other business should greater secrecy be preserved.

15 Spies cannot be usefully employed without a certain intuitive sagacity.

16 They cannot be properly managed without benevolence and straightforwardness.

17 Without subtle ingenuity of mind, one cannot make certain of the truth of their reports.

18 Be subtle! be subtle! and use your spies for every kind of business.

19 If a secret piece of news is divulged by a spy before the time is ripe, he must be put to death together with the man to whom the secret was told.

20 Whether the object be to crush an army, to storm a city, or to assassinate an individual, it is always necessary to begin by finding out the names of the attendants, the aides-de- camp, and door-keepers and sentries of the general in command. Our spies must be commissioned to ascertain these.

21 The enemy's spies who have come to spy on us must be sought out, tempted with bribes, led away and comfortably housed. Thus they will become converted spies and available for our service.

22 It is through the information brought by the converted spy that we are able to acquire and employ local and inward spies.

23 It is owing to his information, again, that we can cause the doomed spy to carry false tidings to the enemy.

24 Lastly, it is by his information that the surviving spy can be used on appointed occasions.

25 The end and aim of spying in all its five varieties is knowledge of the enemy; and this knowledge can only be derived, in the first instance, from the converted spy. Hence it is essential that the converted spy be treated with the utmost liberality.

26 Of old, the rise of the Yin dynasty was due to I Chih who had served under the Hsia. Likewise, the rise of the Chou dynasty was due to Lu Ya who had served under the Yin.

27 Hence it is only the enlightened ruler and the wise general who will use the highest intelligence of the army for purposes of spying and thereby they achieve great results. Spies are a most important element in water, because on them depends an army's ability to move.